Contents

Introduction

When we began team teaching, we wanted to meet the auditory, visual, and kinesthetic learning styles of our students. We discovered that a combination of music, print, and movement turned out to be effective.

Over the years, we've taught students in all elementary grades, as well as multiage groups, whose readiness and academic abilities have run the gamut from students with special needs to children who are highly gifted. We've found that music is an avenue to learning for all demographics. It has helped strengthen our students' self-esteem, class participation, social interactions, and academic learning. We think you'll find our approach to be fun and beneficial and that the gains are long lasting.

This book provides you with a resource to teach grammar concepts, beginning with parts of speech and progressing through writing development. The 21 mnemonic songs in the collection help students retain language arts skills they need to become stronger readers and writers and to meet English language arts standards. Our original songs are written for students in grades 3–6 and are set to familiar tunes, such as "Alouette," "London Bridge," and "Old MacDonald."

Paired with each song are lesson ideas for adding movement, playing learning games, integrating literature, and extending the song into the content areas. With the songs and follow-up lessons, you have a compelling way to help students learn, recall, and master grammar. Let the music be your guide!

HOW TO USE THIS BOOK

Begin by having students think about how music can be a valuable learning tool. Invite volunteers to sing songs they know by heart. Talk about the power of music and movement in helping commit things to memory. Explain that the class will be learning mnemonic songs, with lyrics specifically written about language arts.

Introducing the Songs

Choose mnemonic songs suited to your class needs. Once you've selected a song, you can present it in a variety of ways. Here are some suggestions:

♪ Play a game of Tune Trivia before teaching the song. Play the tune without any lyrics. You may choose to use a Web site that has the music (see Helpful Web Sites, at left), hum the tune, or, if this is an option, use an instrument such as a guitar, keyboard, or even a kazoo. See if students recognize the song. Once students identify the tune, have the class sing the original song.

SCHOLASTIC

Memory-Boosting Mnemonic Songs
Grammar

20 Fun Songs Set to Familiar Tunes With Engaging Activities That Make Grammar Rules Really Stick

Pat Walz and Pam McLaughlin

New York • Toronto • London • Auckland • Sydney
Mexico City • New Delhi • Hong Kong • Buenos Aires

Teaching Resources

Dedication

With much appreciation to our husbands, Ray and Jack, and our children, Clint, Doug, Chad, and Cassie, who believed in us, encouraged us, and supported us.

Acknowledgments

We would like to thank Sue Lubeck, who championed our ideas and was our advocate for writing this book.

Editor: Sarah Longhi
Content editing by Nicole Iorio
Cover design by Jason Robinson
Interior design by Holly Grundon
Illustrations by Mike Moran

ISBN-13: 978-0-545-14410-0
ISBN-10: 0-545-14410-8

Display the song lyrics on an overhead or an interactive whiteboard. Invite volunteers to hum the first verse or the chorus to pick up the tune. Then, as a group, clap or tap out the rhythm. When the class is ready, sing the first verse aloud. Invite volunteers to examine the lyrics in each verse. As a group, learn and practice singing the song together. Refer to the Tips for Teaching the Song on the Lesson Ideas page so that students can add movement or gestures as they sing.

Give each student a copy of the song. Read the lyrics and discuss the concepts. As a group, practice the song and gestures suggested on the Lesson Ideas page. If you would like to add student-inspired movements, elicit ideas that the group can use as you read and discuss the concepts. Then practice the song and new gestures together.

Begin with literature. Read aloud from a personal favorite that teaches the grammar concept that is your current focus. You may also use the book listed in the Literature Connections on the Lesson Ideas page. After an interactive read-aloud, transition into teaching the related song. Draw connections between the words in the book and those in the song. While you have the attention of the whole class, direct students to the lyrics on an overhead or interactive whiteboard. Model the entire song for the students.

Practicing the Songs

Remember, the goal of this book is to help students learn mnemonic devices. Be sure to set aside time a few days a week for students to practice. Here are some suggestions:

Have students focus on memorizing the initial verse or verses of the song during one lesson. Return the following day to review. Sing one verse repeatedly, and then build on it. Point out to students that the additional verses help them gain advanced knowledge. In the Skills section of Lesson Ideas, you'll find that the skills in some songs can be broken down by verse. You may want to teach only the Basic verses at one point and extend to the Advanced verses later.

Vary student groupings. You may wish to begin and finish with whole-group practice, but also give students time to work separately. Have students read and study the lyrics individually. Also have them practice with partners. Students can work in small groups to rehearse the song.

If students are self-conscious about singing, have them echo phrases of the song after you sing (or say) each one aloud. Allow students to rhythmically say or chant the verses rather than sing them. Also read verses chorally and have small groups try chanting them together without looking at the lyrics. As students become acquainted with the routine, encourage them to sing along.

A Research-Based Approach

Using familiar tunes as mnemonic devices is an effective learning strategy that can help students of all abilities.

Scaffold Learning

"A mnemonic device provides a structure for learning or acquiring information, a series of organizing factors to ensure durable retention, and effective cues for retrieval of the memorized information" (Ashcraft, 1989, pp. 195–196).

Improve Performance

"Memory as it interacts with mastery of educational content is an important process which affects academic success" (Gfeller, 1982, p. 5).

Construct Knowledge

"For many LD students, mnemonic instruction may represent the only realistic chance they will comprehend specific academic content . . ." (Scruggs and Mastropieri, 1990, p. 277).

Resources

Ashcraft, M. H. (1989). *Human memory and cognition*. New York: HarperCollins.

Gfeller, K. E. (1982). The use of melodic-rhythmic mnemonics with learning disabled and normal students as an aid to retention (Doctoral dissertation, Michigan State University). *University Microfilms International*, No. 8303786.

Scrugg, T. E. and Mastropieri, M. A. (1990). Mnemonic instruction for students with learning disabilities: What it is and what it does. *Learning Disability Quarterly, 13*, 271–279.

Further Reading

To learn more about the benefits of using music as a multisensory approach to teaching, look for articles on the subject. You might begin with reading:

Gfeller, K. (1983). Musical mnemonics as an aid to retention with normal and learning-disabled students. *Journal of Music Therapy, 20*(4), 179–189.

Kilgour, A. R., Jakobson, L. S., and Cuddy, L. L. (2000). Music training and rate of presentation as mediators of text and song recall. *Memory & Cognition, 28*(5), 700–710.

Wallace, W. (1994). Memory for music: Effect of melody on recall of text. *Learning, Memory, and Cognition, 20*(6), 1471–1485.

Expanding on the Skills

The first song in the book, "Speech Splash," introduces grammar and may serve as a starting point or review for teaching parts of speech. Each of the 20 songs that follow has an accompanying page of Lesson Ideas. The point of these ideas is to spark students' interest in language arts and to help them lock in what they've learned in the songs. You'll find the following features on each Lesson Ideas page:

- **Skills:** Look here for connections to your English language arts curriculum. Use this section to identify which grammar skills you want to teach, and choose the order in which to introduce the songs.

- **Tips for Teaching the Song:** Movement is a mnemonic connection to the body and the brain. It is key for kinesthetic learners. Use this section to find ideas for adding simple gestures and movements to the song that will help students remember concepts, as well as make the practice playful. Whether you use the suggestions we give or make up your own, use the movements consistently each time you and your students sing the song.

- **Lesson Connections:** This section provides at least two different opportunities for students to actively apply the target skill, including games and activities that require reasoning skills, multisensory techniques that develop students' understanding, and ideas for weaving grammar into literature study. Some of the suggestions here can help you assess whether students have attained mastery of the language arts skill.

- **Curriculum Connections:** For each song, use the extension to another curricular subject. You'll find simple ideas for connecting the grammar skill to math, science, social studies, or art.

- **Literature Connections:** At least one book is suggested to support each song. Look here to find an idea for literature you may want to gather in advance. Always feel free to replace or supplement the suggested titles with favorite books from your collection that support the target skill.

Speech Splash

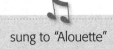

sung to "Alouette"

Verbs show action or they might be linking.
Noun is a name for a person, place, or thing.
Pronouns will replace a noun.
Adjectives describe a noun.

Parts of speech, parts of speech,
Parts of speech, parts of speech,
O-o-o-oh

Soon, all eight of them, we'll learn to say, hey!
We will use them each and every day.

Connecting words are always called *conjunctions*.
Prepositions introduce a phrase.
Adverbs tell where, when, or how.
Interjections are like, "Wow!"

Parts of speech, parts of speech,
Parts of speech, parts of speech,
O-o-o-oh

Now, all eight of them, we know to say, hey!
We will use them each and every day.

noun-Sense

sung to "Three Blind Mice"

A noun is a name
For a person, place, or thing.
A noun is a name
For a person, place, or thing.

Oh, *cowboy*'s the name of a person. Ta-da!
And *ranch* is the name of a place. Uh-huh!
And *horse* is the name of a thing. Ye-haw!
A person, place, or thing. (Yeah!)*

A common noun (like *cowboy*!)*
Is person, place, or thing.
A proper noun (like *Shane*!)*
Is a special noun.

Use capital letters for proper nouns:
Titles, names, important works.
Proper nouns need capitals.
Use capitals! (Yeah!)*

*Whispered and spoken part

"Noun-Sense" Lesson Ideas

Skills

Basic: Identify a noun as a word that names a person, place, or thing (Verse 1).

Advanced: Recognize common and proper nouns (Verse 2).

Tips for Teaching the Song

Invite students to focus on key words for identifying a noun by using actions and gestures as they sing. Have them try these movements or make up your own.

- For *person*, tip an imaginary hat as you say "Ta-da!"

- For *place*, extend a hand in front of your chest, palm up, and gesture from left to right.

- For *thing*, circle an arm in the air as if to rope cattle with a lariat and say: "Yee haw!"

- For the last phrase in the first verse, touch hands to head for *person*, to waist for *place*, and to toes for *thing*.

- For *Yeah!*, have students make a celebratory gesture.

Lesson Connections

1 Hand out copies of the song or display it on-screen. Ask students to highlight words in the song that represent people, places, or things.

2 Brainstorm additional nouns and write them on index cards. Have students sort the word cards into the categories Person, Place, or Thing. (Basic) Have students sort the word cards into the categories Common Nouns and Proper Nouns. (Advanced)

3 Choose two teams to play Noun Bee, a spelling bee–type game, using the noun word cards from Step 2 and any additional nouns collected from students' reading. On each turn, you present a noun card. Two players—one from each team—compete to identify whether the noun on the card is a person, place, or thing (Basic) or is common or proper (Advanced). The first player to give a correct answer wins a point for his or her team.

Curriculum Connections (Math): Organize students into groups of three or four. Have the groups scan current events articles to see how many nouns they can collect in five minutes (on scrap paper, they can sort the nouns by category in columns). Ask students to make a bar graph that compares the number of words they found in each noun category. Guide students to write mathematical equations comparing the results of the graph, such as using greater-than or less-than symbols (e.g., "25 (people) > 14 (places) + 10 (things)").

Literature Connections: Choose current events articles, student writing, or picture books that contain a variety of common and proper nouns. One of our favorite picture books for this lesson is *Bubba the Cowboy Prince: A Fractured Texas Tale,* by Helen Ketteman, a humorous Cinderella parody that presents all types of nouns—with a southwestern flair.

Vivacious Verbs

sung to "Old MacDonald"

V-E-R-B-S

Many verbs are action words—
    V-E-R-B-S.
Verbs tell things that you can do—
    V-E-R-B-S.
With a run, jump here
And a hop, skip there,
Here a dance, there a leap,
Then we all go to sleep.
Verbs you know are action words—
    V-E-R-B-S.

Many verbs are action words—
    V-E-R-B-S.
Verbs tell things that you can do—
    V-E-R-B-S.
With a twist, twirl here
And a push, pull there,
Here a smile, there a frown,
Then we all can sit down.
Verbs you know are action words—
    V-E-R-B-S.

Sometimes verbs are linking verbs—
    V-E-R-B-S.
Link subjects with their predicates—
    V-E-R-B-S.
With a subject here,
A predicate there,
Here a was, there a were,
Choose a linking verb, yes, sir!
Sometimes verbs are linking verbs—
    V-E-R-B-S.

Sometimes verbs are linking verbs—
    V-E-R-B-S.
Link subjects with their predicates —
    V-E-R-B-S.
With a subject, Grace
Add a small link, is
Tells "to be" and that's not all.
Grace is really very tall.
Sometimes verbs are linking verbs—
    V-E-R-B-S.

Sometimes verbs are helping words—
    V-E-R-B-S.
They come before the major verb—
    V-E-R-B-S.
With a have, has, did,
And a could, should, would,
They show the time and take the lead.
Helping verbs are what we need!
Sometimes verbs are helping words—
    V-E-R-B-S.

Sometimes verbs are helping verbs—
    V-E-R-B-S.
They come before the major verb—
    V-E-R-B-S.
With a subject, Juan,
Add a helper, has,
Tells the time, when to bake:
Juan has baked a yummy cake.
Sometimes verbs are helping verbs—
    V-E-R-B-S.

"Vivacious Verbs" Lesson Ideas

Skills

Basic: Identify a verb as a word that shows action (Verses 1 and 2).

Advanced: Recognize that linking verbs are words used to connect a subject and a predicate, and helping verbs help show time and are always followed by another verb (Verses 3, 4, 5, and 6).

Tips for Teaching the Song

Guide students to create body sculptures and gestures that accompany the lyrics.

- As is sometimes done with the song "Y.M.C.A.," students can arrange their hands and legs to form the letters for V-E-R-B-S.

- Simulate the actions listed. Students can twist and turn their bodies. They can smile, frown, and sit down. To show *has*, they can pretend to clutch something.

- For *linking verbs*, they can clap their hands to represent a subject and predicate linking.

- For *helping verbs*, students can pat themselves on the back.

Keep in mind that students may need a background understanding of subjects and predicates (see pages 36–37). For more work with verbs, use the Make Sense of Tense lesson on verb tense (see pages 32–33).

Lesson Connections

1 Use shoes to symbolize actions. Have students cut out pictures of shoes or bring in actual shoes, such as cowboy boots, soccer cleats, flippers, slippers, dance shoes, baby shoes, or sandals. Invite students to state or demonstrate an action for a kind of shoe. (Basic)

2 On different sentence strips, write a variety of subjects, adjectives, and linking verbs, such as *is, are, was,* and *were*. Organize students into groups of three. Ask one student to choose a subject, another to choose an adjective, and a third to find an appropriate linking verb to complete the sentence. Have the trio display the complete sentence and read it to the group. (Basic)

3 Prepare subject sentence strips as you did in Step 2. In addition, write a set of sentence strips with simple predicates showing actions in the past tense (*baked a cake, washed the car*), and another set with helping verbs rather than linking verbs. Divide the class into groups of four. Ask one student in each group to identify the main verb on the predicate strip and another student to choose a strip with an appropriate helping verb. Have the other two students put the three strips together to complete the sentence. (Advanced)

Curriculum Connections (Art): Brainstorm lists of action verbs and helping verbs. Have students choose four or five action verbs to include in an illustration. Have students draw pictures and add captions that demonstrate their understanding of how helping verbs can support action verbs. Model by drawing a sketch on the board of two children climbing up a hill. Write: *The girls could climb high.*

Literature Connections: Read a range of texts aloud, including poetry, nonfiction, and picture books to have students listen for different verbs. A picture book that offers a variety of verbs is *Kites Sail High,* by Ruth Heller. Heller's vibrant concept book includes action words, linking verbs, and helping verbs.

Dazzling Describers

sung to "Oh, My Darling, Clementine"

Oh, my adjective, you describe a noun.
You make pictures in my mind.
You tell which one, and how many,
Also, how much and what kind.

Oh, my adjective, you have different forms.
There are three forms we should know:
Positive and comparative
But superlative tops the show.

When, my adjective, you describe one noun
Not a thing will you compare.
Positive is what we call you.
Just one image you can share.

Let's compare two nouns. That's *comparative*.
Syllables help with this chore.
With one syllable, we'll add *e-r*.
With most others, we'll add *more*.

Let's compare more nouns. That's *superlative*.
Three or more, you'll want to boast.
With one syllable, we'll add *e-s-t*.
With more syllables, we'll add *most*.

"Dazzling Describers" Lesson Ideas

Skills

Basic: Identify an adjective as a word that describes a noun, pronoun, or another adjective (Verse 1).

Advanced: Recognize that positive adjectives describe a noun, comparative adjectives compare two nouns, and superlative adjectives describe three or more nouns (Verses 2, 3, 4, and 5).

Tips for Teaching the Song

Add actions and gestures to match certain words. For the first verse, give these directions:

- For *mind,* point to your head.
- For *one,* hold up your index finger.
- For *how many,* touch each finger, as if counting.
- For *how much,* hold open your palms, as if weighing an object.
- For *what kind,* gesture making different shapes.

Have students collaboratively make up movements or gestures for the rest of the song.

Lesson Connections

1. Read *The Great Kapok Tree,* by Lynne Cherry, or another book full of colorful adjectives, and compose a class list of adjectives. Supplement the list as students learn more adjectives. (Basic)

2. Give students pictures of animals and have them compare the animals by writing sentences with adjectives. Example 1: *The frog is small.* Point out that *small* is a positive adjective. (Basic) Example 2: *The poison arrow frog is smaller than the ocelot.* Explain that the comparative adjective *smaller* contrasts the frog and the ocelot. Note that the suffix *-er* is added to one-syllable adjectives, whereas *more* usually precedes those with two or more syllables. (Advanced) Example 3: *The poison arrow frog is the smallest frog I know.* The superlative adjective *smallest* compares the specific frog to other frogs. Point out that the suffix *-est* is usually added to one-syllable adjectives, whereas *most* precedes many, but not all, adjectives with two or more syllables. (Advanced)

3. Invite students to design a "wanted" poster in which they describe a chosen topic, animal, or character with writing that contains specified adjective forms. (Advanced)

Curriculum Connections (Science): Divide the class into groups of four to six to research animal habitats. Have each group collaboratively design a project, such as a diorama or mural, and present it to the class using a combination of adjectives.

Literature Connections: Adjectives are found in varied texts, including the lovely picture book *The Great Kapok Tree,* by Lynne Cherry. With lush illustrations and language, readers experience the rain forest and its creatures.

Absolutely Adverbs

sung to "Row, Row, Row Your Boat"

Adverbs describe some verbs—
Adverbs, adjectives, too.
They tell where or when or how
And end in *l-y*, too.

Always, never, soon,
Are adverbs tried and true.
Merrily, carefully, weekly, quickly—
You just sang a few.

Adverbs come in different forms.
Three that you should know:
Positive, and comparative—
Superlative tops the show.

She rows quickly and seriously.

He rows slowly and carefully.

Adverbs that describe one word
Have nothing to compare.
They are all called *positive*.
One image they can share.

Comparative compares two words.
Syllables help this chore.
One syllable, you add *e-r*.
Others, you add *more*.

Superlative compares more words.
Three or more to boast.
One syllable, add *e-s-t*.
More syllables, add *most*.

"Absolutely Adverbs" Lesson Ideas

Tips for Teaching the Song

Have students add facial gestures and body movements to specific words and phrases. Give these directions:

- For *merrily*, smile as you march. For *quickly*, run in place.
- For each use of *comparative*, hold out your arms like a balance scale.
- For both *tops the show* and *most*, raise your arms above your head.

Lesson Connections

1 Read aloud a book with several examples of adverbs, such as Ruth Heller's *Up, Up and Away*. Afterward, have the class create a list of adverbs. Keep this chart displayed and add to it as students learn more adverbs. (Basic)

2 Lead a game of Guess My Rule. On the board, write one verb and a list of adjectives, nouns, and adverbs that describe that verb. Create a two-column chart, listing adverbs on the left and the other words on the right. After students have reviewed the chart and looked at the verb, say: "I am an adverb. Guess my rule!" Students should respond that adverbs describe a verb. Extend the game by categorizing adverbs by whether they describe when, where, or why. (Basic)

3 Brainstorm types of sporting events. Then organize students into groups. Assign each group a sporting event, and have students list verbs related to it. Ask groups to write a sentence that contains a positive adverb, such as *Clint swam fast*. Next, ask groups to compose sentences that use comparative and superlative adverbs, such as *Mia swam faster than I did. Audrey swam the fastest backstroke on the team.* (Advanced)

Curriculum Connections (Social Studies): In small groups, have students write state riddles that have at least two adverbs. The adverbs can describe what people do in the state. Example: *It is better to visit me in summer if you dislike the cold. More polar bears roam happily here than anywhere else in the country. What state am I? (Alaska)* Circulate to check for adverb usage. Have groups exchange their riddles.

Literature Connections: Share picture books that offer adverbs. One good example is *Up, Up and Away,* by Ruth Heller. Heller acquaints readers with adverbs throughout this sensory-rich book.

Skills

Basic: Identify an adverb as a word that describes a verb, an adjective, or another adverb (Verse 1).

Advanced: Recognize that adverbs have different forms (Verses 2, 3). Identify that a positive adverb describes a word without comparing (Verse 4), a comparative adverb compares two verbs or ideas (Verse 5), and a superlative adverb compares three or more verbs or ideas (Verse 6).

Practical Pronouns

sung to "Down by the Station"

When there's a noun,
A pronoun can replace it.
Here are *subject pronouns*
Lined up in a row:
You, I, it, he, or *she*,
Singulars that rename.
Plurals *we, they*—
Off you go!

When there's a noun,
A pronoun can replace it.
Here are *object pronouns*
Lined up in a row:
You, me, it, him, or *her*,
Singulars that rename.
Plurals *us, them*—
Off you go!

When there's a noun,
A pronoun can replace it.
These *possessive pronouns*
Are lined up in a row:
My or *mine*, *ours* or *theirs*,
These words tell who owns it.
Pronouns, pronouns—
Now let's go!

"Practical Pronouns" Lesson Ideas

Tips for Teaching the Song

Model actions for some of the phrases in the song.

♪ For *replace it*, pretend to hold something, then throw it over your shoulder.

♪ For *Off you go!* act as if you are leaving in a hurry.

♪ For *singulars*, hold up one finger and for *plurals*, start with two fingers and then count off the rest of your fingers on two hands.

Lesson Connections

1 Read aloud a selection from a favorite class book that is filled with a variety of pronouns. As students listen, have them make a tally mark for every pronoun they hear. Discuss how many and which pronouns students have heard. Make sure students can tell you what noun the pronoun is replacing (its antecedent). (Basic)

2 Label four paper lunch bags: *nouns, subject pronouns, object pronouns,* and *possessive pronouns*. Fill the noun bag with nouns written on small slips of paper. Announce that a student will pull out a noun and write an appropriate pronoun on the back. Select another student to use that pronoun in a sentence, and then select a final student to place the pronoun in the correct pronoun bag. Repeat. To keep the entire class involved, randomly draw names for the noun selectors. (Advanced)

Curriculum Connections (Math): Point out that pronouns replace nouns as numbers do in algebraic equations. Give examples for students to see the relationship. Students can solve multistep equations by first completing the operation in parentheses, then replacing that step with the equivalent answer (as they would do with a pronoun) before tackling the next part of the equation.

Example 1: $(7 + 3) - 2 = ?$ Replace $(7 + 3)$ with 10. Then $10 - 2 = 8$

Example 2: $(a + b) + c = a + (b + c)$. If $a = 1, b = 2, c = 4$, the equation would be $(1 + 2) + 4 = 1 + (2 + 4)$. Replace the $(1 + 2)$ with 3, and $(2 + 4)$ with 6 so $3 + 4 = 1 + 6 = 7$. In this case the variables act like pronouns.

Literature Connections: To teach about pronouns, read *I and You and Don't Forget Who: What Is a Pronoun?* by Brian P. Cleary. Cleary takes a jovial look at pronouns and their definitions through lively text and illustrations. The pronouns are printed in color and stand out clearly to young readers.

Basic: Identify that pronouns are words used in place of nouns (Verse 1).

Advanced: Recognize that a subject pronoun is used as a subject of a sentence, an object pronoun is used after an action verb or in a prepositional phrase, and a possessive pronoun shows ownership (Verses 2 and 3).

Over, Before, and Through the Phrases

sung to "Over the River"

"*Over* the river" and "*through* the woods,"
Prepositions lead the phrase.
We use them to relate to nouns
With other words in the sentence.
Over, above, through, across, between—
Prepositions lead a phrase.
Add nouns and some describing words—
They'll tell us more always.

"*Before* our lunch" and "*in* the rain."
Prepositions lead the phrase.
Locate things in time or space,
And under what condition.
Before, around, after, with, until—
Prepositions lead a phrase.
Add nouns and some describing words—
They'll tell us more always.

"Over, Before, and Through the Phrases" Lesson Ideas

Tips for Teaching the Song

Emphasize the main concept and the examples of prepositions by adding hand gestures that show directions such as *over, under, through,* and *between*. You might also have students act out the prepositions with objects they can move easily and work with safely, such as small, sturdy blocks or boxes. For *over,* they can step over the block, for *between,* they can walk between two blocks, and so on.

Skills

Basic: Identify a preposition as a word that introduces a phrase ending with a noun.

Advanced: Recognize that a prepositional phrase relates to another noun or pronoun in the sentence.

Lesson Connections

1 After reading aloud a book that contains several prepositional phrases, have students dramatize the story with flannel-board figures or magnetic pictures. Write prepositional phrases on chart paper, and have students underline the prepositions.

2 Compose a list of sentences with prepositional phrases. Group students into two teams to play Prepositional Basketball. Assign a referee to look for talkers. Establish rules in advance. Rules: To score, the "shooter" can choose a free throw worth one point, a lay-up or slam dunk worth two points, or a three-pointer. Responses are weighted in difficulty. After each successful answer, a new player on the team "shoots." If an answer is missed, the opposing team gets possession. If a player on the opposing team talks, the team with the ball gets the rebound and a chance to slam-dunk. That team has possession until it gives a wrong answer. If a player on the shooting team talks, the other team steals the ball. The team with the most points wins. Use the following scale:

> Free Throw: Identify a prepositional phrase in a sentence.
>
> Lay-up: Identify the prepositional phrase and the preposition.
>
> Slam Dunk: Create a new sentence containing the prepositional phrase.
>
> Three-Pointer: Identify all the parts of speech in a prepositional phrase.

Curriculum Connections (Social Studies): Have pairs draw treasure maps based on directions that use prepositional phrases. One student dictates phrases, such as *over the river, through the field, between the trees,* and *into the barn.* The partner sketches the map to match the words. Together, students illustrate their treasure maps.

Literature Connections: Try using a classic Dr. Seuss book that highlights prepositional phrases through rhymes. Read aloud *In a People House,* by Theo LeSieg.

Conjunction Combos

sung to "You're a Grand Old Flag"

You're a *conjunction* if you connect the words.
And, or, but are just some that we know.
There is *and* that informs
While *or* gives a choice.
But will compare more than one.

You're a *conjunction* and you're used all the time.
You will help to expand ideas.
When you're used too much,
You run on and on.
Use conjunctions with careful thought!

"Conjunction Combos" Lesson Ideas

Skills

Identify conjunctions as words such as *and, but, or, for, so, because, since,* and *before* that connect individual words, phrases, or two simple sentences.

Tips for Teaching the Song

To emphasize the concept of conjunctions being connectors, have students leap to their feet and spread their arms out to reach the fingertips of their classmates every time they sing *conjunction* and examples of conjunctions: *and, or, but.*

Lesson Connections

1. Read aloud a few paragraphs from a book of your choice. As you come to conjunctions, say them emphatically. Then call up students to read dramatically, as you've modeled, from their own writing or another text that contains a number of conjunctions.

2. Distribute to student pairs copies of a print article from a student publication, newspaper, or magazine. Have each pair circle conjunctions in the article and then ask pairs to compare their results. Alternatively, have students glue small pieces of elbow macaroni between the conjunctions and the words they connect.

3. Provide two words, phrases, or simple sentences, so students can suggest conjunctions to connect them. Discuss how the conjunction expands a thought. Ask students to justify their answers by explaining the connections.

4. Have student pairs write a list of short sentences that are related to one another. The sentences should not have any conjunctions. Have pairs exchange their lists. Explain that each pair will use conjunctions to combine the sentences they receive or rewrite the sentences to communicate the concepts using conjunctions.

Curriculum Connections (Social Studies): Assign each student a current-events article. Have students report and write about something that has occurred in the school or the community. You may have students write the piece using a predetermined list of conjunctions or revise their writing to include several conjunctions.

Literature Connections: Analyze current-events stories to find various ways that news writers connect thoughts using conjunctions. Also share a book in which the author incorporates numerous conjunctions, such as *Just Me and 6,000 Rats: A Tale of Conjunctions,* by Rick Walton. Walton's playful book weaves conjunctions naturally into the story.

Introducing Interjections

sung to "Pop Goes the Weasel"

"Ow!" is just a single word,
We call an *interjection*.
It states an emotion—how we feel.
Say it with inflection!

"Eek! I see a really big bug!"
The mark's an exclamation.
Use a comma in "Whew, he's gone"—
A weaker situation.

"Introducing Interjections" Lesson Ideas

Skills

Basic: Identify an interjection as a word or short phrase that shows emotion (Verse 1).

Advanced: Recognize that an exclamation mark conveys a strong feeling, whereas a comma is used for a feeling that's less urgent (Verse 2).

Tips for Teaching the Song

Snap your fingers together with the words *Say it* in Verse 1. Clap your hands above your head after *interjection* in Verse 1 and *exclamation* in Verse 2. You may want to use this song as an introduction to teaching "Sentence Sorts" (page 38).

Lesson Connections

1 Read aloud *The Frog Principal,* by Stephanie Calmenson, or choose another picture book that has interesting interjections. Have students repeat the interjections after you and keep count of interjections as they appear in the text. (Basic)

1 Brainstorm interjections that imitate sounds made by people, animals, or things. Explain that such words are called onomatopoeia. Example: "Yeow!" screeched the cat when I stepped on his tail. (Basic)

3 Organize students into small groups. Copy several nursery rhymes for students to read. Have each group think of interjections to use before or after each line. Invite groups to share their results with the class. (Basic) Have students experiment with the position of interjections before, after, or in the middle of a line for effect. (Advanced)

> Example:
>
> Little Miss Muffet
>
> Sat on a tuffet   *Humph!*
>
> Eating her curds and whey.   *Yuck!*
>
> Along came a spider   *Yikes!*
>
> And sat down beside her   *Plop!*
>
> And frightened Miss Muffet away!   *Eek!*

4 Have students work in small groups to write a brief script announcing an event, such as a hockey game or a spring carnival. Explain that it must use at least five interjections. (Advanced)

Curriculum Connections (Social Studies): Have students work in small groups to create and act out a script for a television news broadcast. Direct each group to assign two students to be co-anchors. The other two to four students will be the audience. Have students incorporate audience reactions into the script so that a news anchor says a line and then an audience member responds with an interjection. After they have written their scripts, give groups time to practice. Then invite them to perform for the class.

Literature Connections: Children will enjoy *The Frog Principal,* by Stephanie Calmenson. It is a parody adapted from the classic "Frog Prince" and is full of interjections.

Capitalization Capers

Choose a capital letter
When you write a name.
The first word in a sentence
Always starts the same (with an
    uppercase).
Proper nouns are so specific,
A place, a thing, or name.
Even proper adjectives,
With caps, they start the same.

Chorus

Capitals now.
Capitals wow!
    They start key words. Oh, yes, indeed!
Capitals now.
Capitals wow!
    Use them to succeed.

Bridge

Capitals are important,
Many rules to know-o-o-o—
Capitals are important,
Ready, set, off we go!
And singing,
Fee, fie, fiddle-e-i-o,
Fee, fie, fiddle-e-i-o-o-o,
Fee, fie, fiddle-e-i-o,
Ready, set, off we go!

Choose a capital letter,
For geographic names.
Events that come from history
Also start the same.
Words for names that are so special,
Like "Mom" to replace her name,
Titles such us Mayor Webb,
With caps, they start the same.

Chorus (*repeat*)

Choose a capital letter,
For month, day, holiday names.
Abbreviation of titles,
Like "Dr." starts the same.
Salutations need attention,
Greetings before a name,
Closings in your letters,
With caps, they start the same.

Chorus (*repeat*)

Bridge

Capitals are important,
Many rules to know-o-o-o—
Capitals are important,
Ready, set, off we go!

"Capitalization Capers"
Lesson Ideas

Skills

Identify that a capital letter is used with a proper noun, a proper adjective, and the first word of a sentence (Verse 1); recognize that a capital letter is used with geographic names, historical events, personal titles, and pronouns that replace specific names (Verse 2); understand that a capital letter is used for months, days, holidays, title abbreviations, and greetings and closings in letters (Verse 3).

Note: You may want to review "Noun-Sense" (pages 8–9) to ensure that students understand proper and common nouns.

Tips for Teaching the Song

Point out that in the first verse, the phrase in parentheses, *with an uppercase*, should be shouted. Also add gestures to the chorus and bridge.

- For *Capitals now*, have students pound their fists.

- For *Capitals wow*, have them fist pump with both arms as if cheering.

- Model bending down to stand in a sprinter's starting position and beginning a race for *Ready, set, off we go,* and pretending to play a fiddle for *Fee, fie, fiddle-e-i-o.*

Lesson Connections

1 Display a short newspaper article on the overhead or an interactive whiteboard. Distribute copies to students. Discuss and circle capitalized words in the text. Then create a class chart to categorize the capitalizations. In one column, list the first words of sentences. In the next columns, list names and pronoun names, historical events, geographic names, and dates. Discuss the purpose of the article's capital letters. (Basic)

2 Play Rapid Fire, a quick thinking game. Each student needs a sheet of paper and a pencil. Give students a variety of categories and challenge them to list as many related proper nouns as they can. For example, announce *businesses* as the category. Give students one minute to write as many proper nouns about businesses as they can. Then pair students to compare and expand their combined lists for two additional minutes. Next, have each pair of students join another pair to repeat the compare-and-combine process for another two minutes. At the end, have each group tally the total number of proper nouns they listed and then elicit unique responses from each group to share with the class. (Advanced)

Curriculum Connections (Social Studies): Invite students to select a country and design travel brochures that include places of interest, best dates to visit, and some cultural information. Emphasize the importance of using capitalization conventions for all geographic names. Provide a printed travel brochure as a model.

Literature Connections: There is a wide range of books with ample examples of capitalizations. One that students will enjoy is *The Worst Band in the Universe,* by Graeme Base. This book sparks student imaginations to explore many uses of proper nouns while showcasing capitalization.

25

Talking Twosomes

sung to "The Wheels on the Bus"

Quotation marks are talking marks.
They come in pairs, when people talk,
A pair to start and a pair to stop—
Use quotation marks.

Quotation marks have several jobs.
They're used for titles of many works,
Short stories, songs, and poems, too—
Use quotation marks.

Start a quote with a capital.
Put one where the quote begins.
Don't forget to punctuate
Inside quotation marks.

Dialogue in quotation marks
Sometimes halts when writers talk.
Commas split up these two parts
Inside quotation marks.

Another job for quotation marks:
Surround a quote from someone's work.
Extract a part, not all of it—
Use quotation marks.

Title words and talking marks—
Quite a job for quotation marks.
A pair to start and a pair to stop—
Use quotation marks.

26

"Talking Twosomes" Lesson Ideas

Tips for Teaching the Song

Every time the words *quotation marks* are sung, make air quotes with your fingers. Repeat this action, using your right hand for *starting quotes* and left hand for *ending quotes* in verse 3.

Lesson Connections

1 Read aloud "Goldilocks and the Three Bears" or another familiar story that has memorable speech. Stop to point out the dialogue. Ask students to stand when a quotation begins and sit when it ends.

2 Play Order It, a movement game. Divide the class into small groups. Give each group a set of word cards that form a sentence containing a quotation. Shuffle the cards. Example: *cried, porridge, my, ate, someone, Papa Bear.* Ask students from each group to line up and display their words in the correct order. Have remaining students twist their bodies to form quotation marks and stand in the proper places. Alternatively, students can make air quotes or hold up index cards that show quotation marks.

3 With students' help, generate a list of titles of short stories, poems, and songs. Ask students to choose a title and write a paragraph that describes or reviews the story, poem, or song. Remind students to use proper punctuation (check for proper placement of quotation marks around the title of the text under discussion).

4 Help students find a picture book that is told entirely through narration, such as *If You Give a Mouse a Cookie,* by Laura Numeroff. Ask students to work in pairs to retell the story, adding dialogue between characters. Check students' work as they write, to see that they are correctly using quotation marks.

5 Have pairs of students read a nonfiction book or article and choose three important facts to quote. Have the pairs write their favorite quote in the context of a sentence that they can share with the class. You might provide a frame for the sentence, such as *If you read* [title], *you'll learn amazing facts about* [topic], *like* "[quotation]."

Curriculum Connections (Art): Have students work in teams to design a print advertisement for an imaginary product. Direct each team to create an appealing design for their ad, which can include illustrations, printed images from online research, and photos cut from magazines. Students should work collaboratively to generate a slogan or testimonials for their ad, using quotation marks. Have teams present their ads.

Literature Connections: Share comic books and picture books with vivid dialogue. Read aloud *The Honest-to-Goodness Truth,* by Patricia C. McKissack to not only teach the proper use of quotation marks but also discuss a young girl's lesson about the power of her words.

Lofty Apostrophe

sung to "My Bonnie Lies Over the Ocean"

Apostrophes are very useful.
In contractions, they're letters left out.
In possessives, they help tell who owns it,
But used with a plural, look out!

Chorus
Apostrophe, Apostrophe—
Contractions, possessives are where they'll be.
Apostrophe, Apostrophe—
In regular plurals, you won't see.

Apostrophes are very useful.
They look like commas up high.
They make your writing so easy.
So practice and give them a try!

Chorus (*repeat*)

"Lofty Apostrophe" Lesson Ideas

Tips for Teaching the Song

Focus on the varied functions of an apostrophe by adding gestures to the first verse.

- For *they're letters left out,* hold your hands to your forehead to look for something.

- For *they help tell who owns it,* hug yourself and say "Mine!"

- Wag your finger for *with a plural, look out!*

Skills

Identify that an apostrophe looks like a raised comma and that it is used in contractions to combine two words and in possessives.

Lesson Connections

1 Have students work in pairs to search through magazines for text that uses apostrophes. Ask pairs to cut out as many examples as they can find. Then, have them sort the words into the categories *contractions* and *possessives.* Discuss an additional category to look for: *special plurals.* Point out that plurals of a letter, a number, or a sign may use apostrophes.

2 Play a game of Apostrophe Baseball using examples of contractions, possessives, and plurals that will help students review what they've learned:

- Divide the class into two teams. Set up four bases (locations) in your classroom. Assign an umpire to watch for talkers.

- Explain the rules: A player from the first team is up. He or she can choose an example that is valued as a single, double, or triple. (The examples you've prepared should be weighted in difficulty.) If the player answers correctly, he or she moves to the appropriate base. Play continues, and students move around the bases as in a baseball game. Teams receive a point each time a player reaches home plate. If a player answers incorrectly, the team has an out. After three outs or all the players on the team have been up (whichever comes first), the opposing team gets up. If there is any talking or interrupting by the opposing team, the team at bat gets to advance one base. If the batting team talks, it is penalized with one out.

- To write examples at the appropriate level, follow these tips: Single: simple contractions and plural numbers, letters, and signs (example: *I have two a's in my name*). Double: singular possessives (example: *Pat's bike is red*). Triple: plural possessives (example: *The boys' bikes are new*).

Curriculum Connections (Math): Note that commas in numbers function like apostrophes in contractions. They represent something. The commas hold places to separate the hundreds from the thousands, the thousands from the millions, and so on. Give student pairs large numbers without any commas and ask them to insert them. After writing commas, have them write what places each comma separates. Then give pairs contractions in which they circle each apostrophe and write the letter or letters it represents.

Literature Connections: Share a picture book that explicitly teaches about apostrophes. *Greedy Apostrophe: A Cautionary Tale,* by Jan Carr makes grammar playful and motivates students to learn apostrophe tricks.

Just One or More

Singular means it is just one—
Just one, just one.
Plurals mean it's two or more.
Hundreds, thousands—don't ignore.

When there's more, you add an *s*—
Plurals, plurals.
Ones, tens, hundreds, thousands, too—
Even just a few.

Bridge 1
Special letters to watch
Don't just add an *s*
C-h, *s-h*, *s*, or *x*
You must add *e-s*!

Words that end in consonant *y*,
Change them, change them.
Change *y* to *i*, then add *e-s*.
Vowel *y*, just add an *s*!

Words that end in vowel *o*,
Add *s*, add *s*.
Consonant *o* needs special care—
You must add *e-s*.

Bridge 2
Singular and plurals
Are in much demand.
These few rules can help you spell.
Now you understand.

When *f* becomes plural, but sounds like *v*
Change it, change it
Change *f* to *v*, then add *e-s*
Hear an *f*, then just add *s*.

Exceptions will not follow rules
Learn them, learn them
Nouns we call irregular—
Know these words sometimes occur.

Bridge 2 (*repeat*)

"Just One or More" Lesson Ideas

Tips for Teaching the Song

Model how to add gestures for all the phrases that replace *doo-da* in the original song.

- For *just one*, hold up your pointer finger, signaling number 1.

- For *plurals*, hold your hands in front of you as if you are carrying many things.

- For *change them* and *change it*, gesture unscrewing a light bulb and throwing it out.

- For *add s*, skywrite an *s* and for *learn them*, tap your head.

Lesson Connections

1 Play Guess My Rule. Provide a list of singular words and plural words that end in *s*. Write the words into two columns with singulars in one column and their plurals in the other. Have a volunteer guess the rule. Vary the game by listing singular words that end in *ch, sh, ss, x,* or *s* and their plurals. For a third round, use singular words ending in consonant *y* and their plurals. (Basic) For the fourth and fifth rounds, choose singular words ending in *o* and *f* and their plurals. (Advanced)

2 Have students work in pairs to review a printed article or book excerpt. Be sure that the selections you hand out have a variety of examples of nouns. Ask each pair to circle all the singular nouns on the page. Have them exchange papers with another pair. Then have students write a list of the singular nouns found and the corresponding plurals. (Advanced)

Curriculum Connections (Science): Initiate group explorations of animal species: mammals, birds, reptiles, and amphibians. Ask students to compile a list of animals for a chosen group within the category, using plural names for each animal. For example, students might list forest animals as *bears, foxes, buffaloes, elk calves,* and *deer.* Take the opportunity to discuss exceptions to the plural rules, as in *deer.*

Literature Connections: To emphasize plural nouns, read aloud *"Galápagos" Means "Tortoises,"* by Ruth Heller. Heller's lively rhymes educate readers about sea creatures in the Galápagos. Her use of animal names can be a springboard to singular and plural noun study.

Skills

Basic: Identify that singular nouns refer to one and plural nouns refer to two or more. Identify that plurals usually have an *s* added, while words ending in *ch, sh, x,* or *s* are formed by adding *es* (Verses 1 and 2). Recognize that plurals that end with a consonant before a *y* are formed by changing the *y* to an *i* and adding *es,* while plurals that end with a vowel before the *y* are formed by adding an *s* (Verse 3).

Advanced: Understand that plurals that end with a consonant before an *o* are formed by adding *es,* while plurals that end with a vowel before an *o* are formed by adding an *s* (Verse 4). Recognize that singular nouns that end in *f* but that sound like *v* as plurals are formed by changing the *f* to *v* and adding *es,* and singular nouns that end in *f* and sound like *f* as plurals are formed by adding an *s* (Verse 5).

Make Sense of Tense

Times for verbs help make sense.
Past, present, future are labeled tense.
Use an action verb, a helping verb, or both.
Regular verbs are used the most.

Present tense happens now.
In the barn, Sam milks the cow.
Note the action verb, *milks*. It shows you the time.
With present tense, your grammar's fine.

Past tense comes before now.
Yesterday Sam milked the cow.
Note the action verb, *milked*. It shows you the time.
With past tense, your grammar's fine.

Future tense, after now—
Later Sam will milk the cow.
Note the helping verb, *will*. It shows you the time.
With future tense, your grammar's fine.

Now you know, verbs make sense,
Past, present, future are labeled tense.
Subjects and verbs, they always must agree.
When they do, you're worry free.

"Make Sense of Tense" Lesson Ideas

Tips for Teaching the Song

In verses 2, 3, and 4, have students add movement to distinguish between the present, past, and future. When they sing *present*, have them point to the floor. For *past*, have students lean back and wave their arms behind their heads. For *future*, have them lean forward and simulate a rocket launch.

Lesson Connections

1 Play a game of Flyswatter. In advance, gather sentences that have different verb tenses. Students can cut sentences from newspapers or magazines, or you can write your own sentences on index cards. Divide the class into two teams. Assign a scorekeeper to keep score and to watch for talkers. Write "Past," "Present," and "Future" on the board in large print. Have one student from each team stand adjacent to one another, each with a flyswatter in hand. Read aloud a sentence. The first student to swat the label of the correct verb tense on the board wins the challenge. The two students go to the back of their teams' lines and two new students begin. Each correct response gets a point. Award additional points to the opposing team if anyone talks or blurts out an answer. (Basic)

2 Vary Flyswatter. This time, write "Correct Agreement" and "Incorrect Agreement" on the board. Write sentences, some with correct and some with incorrect subject-verb agreements. As you read each sentence, ask students from opposing teams to slap the appropriate agreement choice. If *incorrect agreement* is slapped, give the student the opportunity to correct the sentence and receive a second point. (Advanced)

3 Have students conduct peer interviews in which partners ask each other to compare their favorite activities as young children and their favorite activities now. Have each student write a brief compare-and-contrast paragraph about his or her partner based on these interview responses. Ask students to exchange drafts to check for subject-verb agreement. (Advanced)

Curriculum Connections (Science): Assign small groups to research and create a poster depicting an invention or technological advancement. Ask each group to include three scenes: from the past, present, and future. For example, a student could focus on changes in air travel. The poster should include captions and a time line, with complete sentences that include correct verb tense and subject-verb agreement.

Literature Connections: Offer a variety of books with verbs in the past, present, and future tenses. Read aloud the classic *Brave Irene,* by William Steig. Steig writes about Irene's challenging encounter using colorful verbs, mainly in the past tense. Students can write a story extension, using future verbs.

notable-nyms

sung to "Mexican Hat Dance"

Some words are tricky for you and me.
The way that we use them becomes the key.
Spelling and meanings are not just whims—
Antonyms, synonyms, homonyms!

Antonyms are opposites, you see.
There's *hot* or *cold*, and there's *he* or *she*.
There's *in* or *out*, and there's *sink* or *swim*.
In other words, they are antonyms!

Synonyms are similar, you see.
There's *little* and *small* and there's *tiny* and *wee*.
There's *gloomy* and *dark* and there's *dull* and *dim*.
In other words, they are synonyms!

Homonyms are more alike, you see.
There's *to*, *two*, and *too* and *tea* and *tee*.
There's *record* and *record* and *him* and *hymn*.
In other words, they are homonyms!

Two kinds of homonyms you may see.
Homophones are heard like *flea* and *flee*.
Homographs are seen like *lie* and *lie*.
Homonyms are tricky words—Oh, my!

"Notable-nyms" Lesson Ideas

Tips for Teaching the Song

Model actions. For each antonym example in Verse 2, put out one open palm and then the other to indicate "on the one hand" and "on the other" (keep your hands far apart). For examples of synonyms in Verse 3, use a similar gesture, except keep your hands close together. For homonyms (including homophones and homographs) in Verses 4 and 5, clap your hands and keep them held together.

Lesson Connections

1 Pair students to play Antonym Flash. Give each student eight index cards. One student writes a word that has an opposite and holds it up. The other student must quickly write a corresponding antonym. Repeat, having partners alternate roles. When pairs finish the game, have them use their cards to play a matching memory game. (Basic)

2 Vary the procedure to play Synonym Flash. Students may continue using the antonym cards but write compatible synonyms in response to the card their partner holds. (Basic)

3 With student input, create a class list of homophones and homographs. Then invite students to use different forms of word play. Have students write and illustrate puns, riddles, or silly poems. For example, a student could illustrate a woman with a rabbit on her head with the caption: "I can't do a thing with my hare!" The student might write the homophone *hair* on the back of the page. Allow time for students to share their work and find the hidden homonyms. (Advanced)

Curriculum Connections (Art): Have students create pictures to represent examples of all the "-nyms." Model choosing an antonym pair and folding a sheet of paper in half. On the top of one side, write one word from the pair. Draw a picture of it and use the word in a complete-sentence caption. On the other side, repeat with the other word.

Literature Connections: Introduce "-nyms" with books written by Brian P. Cleary, including *Stop and Go, Yes and No: What Is an Antonym?*, *Pitch and Throw, Grasp and Know: What Is a Synonym?*, and *How Much Can a Bare Bear Bear? What Are Homonyms and Homophones?*.

Skills

Basic: Identify that antonyms are words with opposite meanings (Verse 2); synonyms are words that have similar meanings (Verse 3); homonyms are words that are spelled or sound the same but have different meanings (Verse 4).

Advanced: Distinguish between homophones (words that sound the same but have different spellings and meanings) and homographs (words that are spelled the same but have different meanings and may have different pronunciations (Verses 4 and 5).

Sentence Specifics

Subject tells us what or who,
What or who, what or who.
Subject nouns tell what or who,
Something that is always true.

Predicate—the action part,
Action part, action part.
Predicates with verbs, you know,
Help the sentence start to grow.

"The big white dogs" are subject words,
Subject words, subject words.
"The big white dogs" are subject words.
Subjects tell us what or who.

"Pull the sled"—the action part,
Action part, action part,
The verb is "pull"—now this you know.
Predicates make the sentence grow.

Compound subjects have joined
    words—
Add more nouns, join the words.
Subject nouns tell what or who.
Something that is always true.

Compound predicates have joined
    words—
Add more verbs, join the words.
Predicates have verbs, as you know,
That help the sentence start to grow.

Compound subject: "Chad and Doug,"
Subject words, subject words.
"Chad and Doug" will tell us who,
In this sentence, that is true.

Compound predicate: "run and jump,"
Predicates, predicates.
Verbs like "run" and "jump," you know
Make this sentence really grow.

"Sentence Specifics" Lesson Ideas

Tips for Teaching the Song

In the first verse, add a questioning gesture when you sing *what* and point to yourself and different students for *who*. Have students walk in a circle whenever they sing *action*. Clap each time *join* or *joined* is used. Act out verbs such as *pull, run,* and *jump*.

Lesson Connections

1 Read *Meanwhile Back at the Ranch,* by Trinka Hakes Noble, or a book of your choice to review subjects and predicates. Create a T-chart on the board, listing examples from the text. (Basic)

2 On sentences strips, compose separate subjects and predicates. Shuffle and display the strips. Call on volunteers to find corresponding parts to create sentences. (Basic)

3 Distribute blank sentence strips to pairs of students. Have students work collaboratively to create sentences. Invite pairs to come up to the front and attach one clothespin to the simple subject and another to the simple predicate. Then have the pair cut the strip between the complete subject and predicate. For example, in the sentence *The big white dogs pull the wagon,* cut between *dogs* and *pull.* As a follow-up activity, students who need the review can mix and match these strips, identifying where the subject noun and the predicate verb are. (Basic)

4 Extend Step 3 by having students illustrate compound subjects and predicates. Students can create sentences strips and corresponding illustrations for each part of the sentence, and then cut their sentences into individual words. Each pair can exchange their sentence parts and illustrations with another pair to have them put the sentence in order, checking against the picture, if necessary. (Advanced)

Curriculum Connections (Math): Show that dividing sentences into subject and predicate parts relates to fractions. For example, demonstrate that in the sentence *Cassie rides bikes with Aidan,* the subject is one out of five parts, or 1/5 of the words in the subject, while the predicate is four out of five parts, or 4/5 of the words. Ask students to construct various sentences and name the correlating fractions that compare the subject and the predicate to the sentence whole.

Literature Connections: In almost any narrative story, you can draw attention to subjects and predicates. One picture book to read aloud is *Meanwhile Back at the Ranch,* by Trinka Hakes Noble. Noble contrasts the lives of Elma and Rancher Hicks. While the book is geared toward younger children, all ages can enjoy its story while searching for subjects and predicates.

Basic: Identify that a simple subject is a noun that tells what or who does the action; a simple predicate is a verb that shows this action; a complete sentence has a subject and a predicate.

Advanced: Identify that subjects and predicates may be compound and that there may be two or more subjects or predicates.

Sentence Sorts

sung to "Battle Hymn of the Republic"

There are four kinds of sentences that you will need to know.
Declarative makes a statement and is used the most of all.
A question that you ask is called an interrogative.
These are just so easy to recall.

Chorus
A sentence only comes in four kinds.
A sentence only comes in four kinds.
A sentence only comes in four kinds—
To tell, question, command, or exclaim.

With two more kinds of sentences, you'll really know it all.
Imperatives are commands to tell you when to stand or fall.
Exclamatory, a fancy word—emotions you can show,
Has punctuation that is tall!

Chorus (*repeat*)

"Sentence Sorts" Lesson Ideas

Skills

Identify that there are four kinds of sentences: declarative, interrogative, imperative, and exclamatory; understand that a declarative sentence makes a statement, an interrogative sentence asks a question, an imperative sentence states a command or requests something, and an exclamatory sentence displays strong emotions or surprise.

Tips for Teaching the Song

Incorporate movement when each sentence type is featured in the verse. For declarative, put your hands on your hips and stomp. For interrogative, put your palms up and shrug shoulders. For imperative, extend an arm and point your index finger to signal a command. For exclamatory, clap your hands above your head.

Lesson Connections

1 Choose poems from Shel Silverstein's *Where the Sidewalk Ends* to explore different kinds of sentences. Read aloud the poems, and have students identify the kinds of sentences they hear. Model imperative sentences with "Invitation." Use the quotations in "Pancake" and "The Crocodile's Toothache" to discuss interrogative and declarative sentences. Read "The Fourth" for exclamatory sentences. (Basic)

2 Talk about word parts and roots to teach the four kinds of sentences. Explain by saying that for *declarative*, we hear *declare*, which means to say. For *interrogative*, we can think of the verb *interrogate*, which means to question someone. The English word *imperative* comes from the Latin word *imperatus*, which means imperial. Have students think of a king giving a command. For *exclamatory*, remind students to think about a time when they cried out or said something emphatically—in joy, sadness, anger, or fear. (Basic)

3 Have students work in small groups. Assign each group a type of sentence to find and clip from magazine and newspaper articles. Put all the sentences into a bag. Call up volunteers to pull out a sentence, share it with the class, and decide which type it is. (Basic) Add interesting photos to the bag of sentences. When students pull out a picture, have them write a sentence about it on the board and tell what type it is. (Advanced)

Curriculum Connections (Science): Relate the steps of an experiment to sentence types. The hypothesis is like an interrogative sentence in that it asks a question. A materials list relates to a declarative statement as it declares the supplies. The procedure is like an imperative sentence with its commands for specific steps. A conclusion relates to an exclamatory sentence since the success or failure of an experiment results in strong emotions.

Literature Connections: Try reading aloud stories in children's magazines to point out the different sentence types. Also read aloud picture books and poetry collections, such as *Where the Sidewalk Ends,* by Shel Silverstein. Silverstein's playful poems are ripe for exploration of sentence variety.

Simple Summary

sung to "I'm a Little Teapot"

Who, what, when, where, why, you often spy—
Five *W*'s for you to try.
Find them in a story, news, or show.
To summarize, you're set to go!

Who tells the person the scoop's about.
What tells the topic to figure out.
When reveals the date or exact time
Something occurred—was it a crime?

Where tells the town or even the room.
And these four *W*'s help a summary bloom
When *why* is clear, the more you know.
To summarize, you're set to go!

"Simple Summary" Lesson Ideas

Tips for Teaching the Song

Have students brainstorm a gesture or movement for each of the five *W*'s. For example, they might point to themselves for *who*, put their palms together as if holding something for *what*, pretend to be looking at their wrists or checking handhelds for *when*, turn their heads from side to side as if looking around for *where*, and shrugging with palms up for *why*. Remind students to use gesture each time they sing that *W* word.

Lesson Connections

1 Read Chris Van Allsburg's *The Stranger* or another short mystery book. Begin a chart with the headings "Who," "What," "When," "Where," and "Why." Lead students to identify, categorize, and list facts under the correct heading. Have student work to solve the mystery by reviewing the facts.

2 Using an overhead projector or an interactive whiteboard, display a current-events article. Select students to highlight the five *W*'s in the story. Discuss the importance of each fact to the article and how the writer uses the facts to make the story interesting to readers.

3 Have students use Think-Pair-Share to plan a mystery story that they will write. Before they start, have them complete a five-column chart to determine what the five *W*'s of the mystery will be. After students have drafted their mysteries, have them return to partner work for revising that includes having their partner find and suggest ways to strengthen the use of the five *W* facts.

Curriculum Connections (Social Studies): Have students choose a historical event related to a social studies unit you are working on or have recently completed. Have students research and take notes on the event. Then have them write and illustrate a time line that includes an introductory paragraph in which the five *W*'s are stated.

Literature Connections: Try reading various news articles, as well as mystery books, such as *The Stranger,* by Chris Van Allsburg. Van Allsburg's intriguing mystery requires readers to sleuth the five *W* clues before the mystery is solved and the identity of the stranger is revealed. This beautifully illustrated book engages the reader throughout the text.

Paragraph Paths

sung to "Jolly Old Saint Nicholas"

You can build a paragraph,
If you have a plan.
Choose a topic that you know—
You can take a stand.
Think about how to begin.
Occasions can tell when.
Opinions, questions, facts, or quotes—
Hang on to your pen.

The body of the paragraph,
Supports your topic line.
Reasons, details, facts come next.
Examples help define.
Putting things in order now—
Importance, time, and place.
Transition words will make it smooth—
Labels you can trace.

Now you must complete the task,
Conclusion you will need.
A statement that wraps up the parts
To help your plan succeed.
When you get down to the end,
Conclusion will stand tall.
It summarizes and restates—
Tells the folks "That's all!"

Pause and always make a plan
Before you start to write.
Choose a topic and support—
Conclude to your delight!

"Paragraph Paths" Lesson Ideas

Tips for Teaching the Song

You'll find that the last line of each verse lends itself to gesturing. After singing the song once, have students brainstorm gestures to add for each of these lines.

Lesson Connections

1 Model writing a paragraph. Choose a subject and develop a topic sentence. Example: If the subject is *helping dogs,* the topic sentence could be *Dogs help people with disabilities.* Give each student paper, a graphite pencil, a red pencil, and a blue pencil. Have students use red to copy the topic sentence you've written. Have students write a two- or three-sentence body for the paragraph in graphite. After students have written, elicit their ideas and create a strong body paragraph as a group. Example: *Dogs can be trained to alert hearing-impaired people to sounds like an alarm clock, a doorbell, and a crying baby. They can guide visually impaired people throughout the city by stopping at street corners. They can retrieve objects, open doors, or locate help if needed for people who are physically impaired.* Note that transition words, such as *for example, also,* and *finally,* can be used, and have students help you add some transitions. Guide students to write a concluding sentence in blue. Review the whole paragraph together, creating a strong conclusion for the model paragraph.

2 Have students work in small groups to analyze paragraphs in published articles you've selected from newspapers, magazines, or online sources. Have them circle the topic sentence in red, the body in graphite, and the conclusion in blue.

3 Give students a choice of topics. Have students select a topic and write an organized paragraph about the topic, using the colored pencils to highlight each part.

Curriculum Connections (Social Studies): Copy a news or informative article for students to summarize. Have them write a one-paragraph summary of the article using the three-color strategy explained above to structure the paragraph.

Literature Connections: Point out that expository paragraphs can be found in myths and folktales. Share some examples, including *Anansi and the Moss-Covered Rock,* retold by Eric Kimmel. Kimmel's adaptation about the trickster spider, Anansi, provides a good example of writing structure. It can be a springboard for students to explore and write expository paragraphs.

Skills

Identify that a paragraph is a group of sentences that develops one topic and has three basic parts: the topic sentence, the body, and the conclusion.

Understand that the topic sentence states an occasion or position (Verse 1); the body includes reasons, details, and facts that support the topic sentence (Verse 2); and the conclusion summarizes and restates the topic (Verse 3).

Genre Giants

sung to "Short'nin' Bread"

Readers and writers choose five common forms,
Genres are categories, that's the norm.
Learn all the genres, learn 'em right now.
We're going to show you when and how.

Chorus
Narrative, descriptive, and poetry, too,
Persuasive, expository, all on cue—
With genres, writers can make it clear
What kind of writing they've got here.

Narrative is a story we can tell.
Descriptive writing has detail.
Poetry is a written art.
Imagination plays a vital part.

Chorus (*repeat*)

Persuasive is written to persuade.
Take an action; you've been swayed!
Expository is filled with facts.
Directions and details to the max!

Chorus (*repeat*)

"Genre Giants" Lesson Ideas

Tips for Teaching the Song

Model actions for the chorus. Touch each fingertip of one hand with the index finger of the other when listing each genre type. Pretend you're holding a pen and writing in the air for *writers* and circle your eye with your hand as in a telescope for *make it clear*. Pretend to be reading a book for *readers* and yank on your earlobe for *have a good ear*.

Lesson Connections

1 Bring in and read aloud examples of texts that represent each genre of writing. Then have students visit the school or public library to select a book that clearly fits into one genre. After students read their books, call on volunteers to share a short section. They should read aloud an excerpt to the class and have classmates identify the book's genre. (Basic)

2 Choose a theme that will enable students to experience writing in all five genres. For example, pizza can be a theme. Ask students to write personal *narrative* stories about eating at a pizza parlor. Advise them to include at least one paragraph with *descriptive* details of the senses experienced. Then have students work in pairs to develop *poetic* advertising jingles about their favorite pizza, and with illustrations, their ads should *persuade* others why their pizza choice is the best. For *expository* writing, ask students to write a recipe that includes the steps for making their favorite pizza. (Advanced)

Curriculum Connections (Science): Have students work in small groups to expand on a science unit the class has studied. Assign each group a genre. Have students design a cartoon with corresponding captions that embodies the genre. Ask each group to share their completed work, and call on the audience to label the genre.

Literature Connections: Share various examples of texts for each genre. For narrative, try *Henry's Freedom Box*, by Ellen Levine, about a young slave on his freedom quest. To study descriptive writing, read aloud *Thunder Cake*, by Patricia Polacco. Polacco beautifully describes a babushka who helps her grandchild overcome her fear of thunderstorms. A motivating example of poetry is *The Frogs Wore Red Suspenders*, by Jack Prelutsky, with its rhyming poems that will make students laugh. For persuasive writing, read the clever picture book *Dear Mrs. LaRue: Letters from Obedience School*, by Mark Teague. An expository book with fascinating facts to share is *Tornadoes*, by Luke Thompson.

Skills

Identify a genre as a category of writing with shared traits. Recognize that a narrative tells a personal story; descriptive writing uses vivid details to describe a person, place, or thing; poetry is a form often employing rhyme, repetition, and meter; persuasive writing is used to convince a reader of a point of view; and expository writing relates information, as in explanations, directions, or technical writing.

Resourceful Revisions

sung to "The Eensy Weensy Spider"

Editing is the final step before you say you're through.

Stop! Review, refine, rewrite. That's just what you must do.

Check each part. That's really smart. Make sure there's no snafu.

Oh, these three steps together earn lots of praise for you.

Scrutinize your writing; mistakes you can't allow.

Stop! Review your work and fix it. You know how.

Check your spelling, capitals, and punctuation now.

Oh, grammar's quite important when writing takes a bow.

Polishing up your writing now makes it really shine.

Stop! Refine your work, consider your design.

Check the length of sentences for some you might combine.

Oh, vivid words and phrases you add will sound divine.

Completion's round the corner, so hurry—don't delay!

Stop! Rewrite your work and do it all today.

Check your work again; be sure it's all okay.

Oh, share your work. It's now complete; it's time to shout "Hooray!"

"Resourceful Revisions"
Lesson Ideas

Tips for Teaching the Song

Have students add actions and movement. They should hold out their right arms with palm out for *Stop*, put up three fingers for *three steps*, (Verse 1); bow for *takes a bow* (Verse 2); cup ear for *sound divine* (Verse 3); and jump up for *Hooray!* (Verse 4).

Use this song as a grammar review. Return to previous songs and lessons, as needed.

Lesson Connections

1 Write sample paragraphs that contain spelling errors, lack punctuation and capitalization, and have words in an inappropriate order. Paragraphs may vary in difficulty, depending on student abilities. Example sentence: *dog my lucy did rased into the rode?* Model correcting it to become *My dog, Lucy, raced into the road.* Then have students work in pairs to edit a paragraph. Have students explain their corrections.

2 Play a game of Rewrite and Roll. Post a chart with six options that correspond to the numbers on a die: 1. Add adjectives, 2. Substitute a common or proper noun, 3. Choose a stronger verb, 4. Add adverbs, 5. Vary sentence length, and 6. Change a phrase. Have students work in pairs. Distribute sentences that you've copied from the Literature Connections or another text. Roll a die and ask pairs to review, refine, and rewrite according to the number rolled. Example: If 6 is rolled, the pair might change *walking down the road* to *waltzing down the sidewalk*—a change that shows how a character might lightly and gracefully make his or her way down a city street.

3 Have students share their rewrites from Step 2 in small groups during a time named Huddle Hoopla. Remind students to support their peers with positive comments.

Curriculum Connections (Social Studies): Have students work in small groups to develop lists of content-area vocabulary words, based on units you've studied and books you've read. Give students the opportunity to draw from the lists by taking a piece of expository writing they've drafted and using the words while refining their work.

Literature Connections: Many books can serve as discussion starters and motivation for students to do their own writing. One of our favorites to read aloud is *Nothing Ever Happens on 90th Street*, by Roni Schotter. Schotter's surprising story focuses on a girl who receives writing tips as she tours her neighborhood.

Skills

Identify that editing is the final step in the writing process. Recognize the three components of editing and publishing a finished product: to review is to perfect the mechanics of spelling, punctuation, and grammar; to refine is to enhance the text with varied lengths of sentences and choice of words; and to rewrite is to produce a final, updated edition.

Bibliography of Cited Children's Literature

Base, G. (1999). *The Worst Band in the Universe.* New York: Harry N. Abrams.

Calmenson, S. (2001). *The Frog Principal.* New York: Scholastic.

Carr, J. (2007). *Greedy Apostrophe.* New York: Holiday House.

Cherry, L. (1990). *The Great Kapok Tree.* San Diego, CA: Harcourt Brace Jovanovich.

Cleary, B. P. (2005). *How Much Can a Bare Bear Bear?* Minneapolis, MN: Millbrook Press.

Cleary, B. P. (2004). *I and You and Don't Forget Who.* Minneapolis, MN: Lerner Publishing Group.

Cleary, B. P. (2004). *Pitch and Throw, Grasp and Know.* Minneapolis, MN: Carolrhoda Books.

Cleary, B. P. (2006). *Stop and Go, Yes and No.* Minneapolis, MN: Millbrook Press.

Heller, R. (2000) *"Galápagos" Means "Tortoises."* San Francisco: Sierra Club Books for Children.

Heller, R. (1988). *Kites Sail High.* New York: Grosset and Dunlap.

Heller, R. (1991). *Up, Up and Away.* New York: Grossett and Dunlap.

Ketteman, H. (1997). *Bubba the Cowboy Prince.* New York: Scholastic.

Kimmel, Eric. (1988). *Anansi and the Moss-Covered Rock* (Retold). New York: Holiday House.

LeSieg, T. (1972). *In a People House.* New York: Random House.

Levine, E. (2007). *Henry's Freedom Box.* New York: Scholastic.

McKissack, P. C. (2000). *The Honest-to-Goodness Truth.* New York: Antheneum.

Noble, T. H. (1987). *Meanwhile Back at the Ranch.* New York: Philomel.

Numeroff, L. (1985). *If You Give a Mouse a Cookie.* New York: Harper & Row.

Polacco, P. (1990). *Thunder Cake.* New York: Putnam Books.

Prelutsky, J. (2002). *The Frogs Wore Red Suspenders.* San Diego: HarperCollins.

Schotter, R. (1997). *Nothing Ever Happens on 90th Street.* New York: Orchard.

Silverstein, S. (1974). *Where the Sidewalk Ends.* New York: Harper & Row.

Steig, W. (1986). *Brave Irene.* New York: Farrar, Straus, Giroux.

Teague, M. (2002). *Dear Mrs. La Rue.* New York: Scholastic.

Thompson, L. (2000). *Tornadoes.* New York: Children's Press.

Van Allsburg, C. (1986). *The Stranger.* Boston: Houghton Mifflin.

Walton, R. (2007). *Just Me and 6,000 Rats.* New York: Farrar, Straus, Giroux.